THE
Archive Photographs
SERIES

LEVERSTOCK GREEN
AND
BENNETTS END

Mrs Gladys Shuffrey at Leverstock Green Farm c. 1940.

THE
Archive Photographs
SERIES

LEVERSTOCK GREEN
AND
BENNETTS END

Compiled by
Barbara Chapman

CHALFORD

First published 1996
Copyright © Barbara Chapman, 1996

The Chalford Publishing Company
St Mary's Mill, Chalford,
Stroud, Gloucestershire, GL6 8NX

ISBN 0 7524 0373 7

Typesetting and origination by
The Chalford Publishing Company
Printed in Great Britain by
Redwood Books, Trowbridge

Dressed in Their Sunday Best, c. 1906. Taken against the wall of Holy Trinity Church, this shows some of the village girls who attended Sunday School. Their white pinafores and large hats were typical of the Edwardian era.

Contents

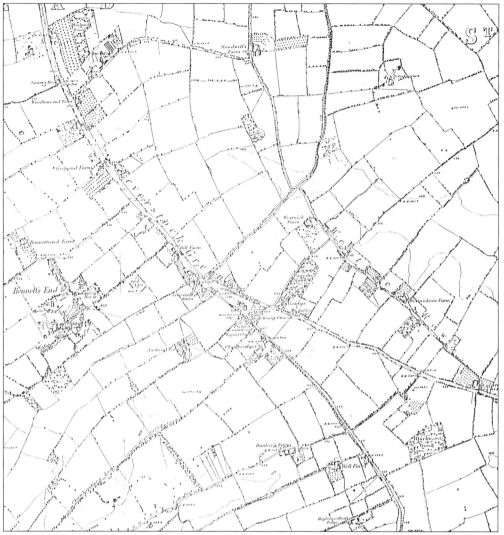

Reduction from the First Edition (1872) Ordnance Survey 6 in:1 mile map, reproduced with the permission of the controller of HMSO, © Crown Copyright.

Introduction

In January 1994, a comment made by archaeologist Mick Aston on Channel 4's *Time Team*, prompted me into researching the history of Leverstock Green where I have lived since 1981. Two years and many hours of study later, research for *The Leverstock Green Chronicle* continues.

It soon became apparent that if I was going to chronicle the history of the area properly, I needed to capture the memories of members of the older generation, before they were lost forever. Interviewing the more elderly members of the community brought with it the delight of seeing their many photographs and postcards. Images of the village and the community as it used to be. By the summer of 1995 this photographic collection had exceeded 250 individual pictures, and I felt they warranted a volume on their own. This book is the result.

A glimpse at a current map shows Leverstock Green to be part of the sprawling New Town of Hemel Hempstead, and to be within the Borough of Dacorum. But Leverstock Green has not always been wholly associated with Hemel, although it's present size is due to its development as one of the New Town's Neighbourhood Communities. Unlike the other neighbourhoods however, Leverstock Green was an existing rural village community at the time of its development, and care was taken to try and retain its village character.

Historically the Leverstock Green area was divided between three parishes: Hemel Hempstead, St Michaels and Abbots Langley. Hemel parish was in the Hundred of Dacorum and the other two in the Hundred of Cashio and the Liberty of St Albans. Even after the establishment of the parish of Leverstock Green, most of the village was outside first the Bailiwick, and then after its Incorporation in 1898, the Borough of Hemel Hempstead.

The roads and lanes of the area, as shown on the 1872 O.S. map (see page 6), date back to the Middle Ages, and in the case of the two main roads, to Roman times. Where the two Roman routes converged, an area of waste, or green, developed. Fortunately most of this infrastructure still remains and can be traced in our modern roads and streets.

Virtually the whole of our area has been under the plough from very early times. The Medieval manor of Westwick corresponded almost exactly with that part of our locality within the parish of St. Michaels. Westwick's boundaries were similar to those of the Roman villa estate of Gorhambury. To the SW of the High Street Green to Bedmond road, Medieval furlong field boundaries were still in place earlier this century, and many are still preserved in our roads and paths. A recent hedgerow survey along the remaining hedge in Chambersbury Lane dates the hedgerow to the early tenth century. The lane was already known to be an ancient one.

During the Middle Ages the road from St Albans was established as the principal route to the growing settlements of Hemel and Berkhamsted. It was known as the Berkhamsted Way or the Berkhamsted Highway. It wasn't until the development of the Turnpike Roads that it became more of a local route.

Although there was no village centred on Leverstock Green during the Middle Ages, (instead the main settlement was at Westwick,) the oldest recorded farmstead we have in the centre of today's village was Stonards. This existed from the thirteenth century to the sixteenth century, and was to be found off Green Lane, just the school side of The Leaside, and roughly in line with the present day White Horse. The farmstead of Roger de Beneyet (or Beneyt), was also recorded in the thirteenth century, giving rise to the name Bennetts End. Its seventeenth-century successor still stands near the Bennetts End roundabout today. It is known as St Nicholas' Nursery.

Westwick is now considered to be a Shrunken Medieval Village. Originally centred around Gorhambury, the focus of settlement had shifted to Westwick Row by the mid-sixteenth century at the latest, and probably much earlier. For many centuries the concentration of individual farmsteads and labourers tenements along or immediately off Westwick Row was the principle focus of settlement and until its demolition in 1633 a great tithe barn was to be found off the Row more or less opposite today's Westwick Warren.

By the beginning of the seventeenth century the whole area was a very prosperous agricultural community, with numerous well-established farmsteads. There was in addition a small brick and tile making industry at Tyle Kiln, situated at the far end of Tile Kiln Lane.

The eighteenth century saw more dwellings, The Leather Bottle, and a smithy appearing around the green – the beginnings of the village of Leverstock Green. Prior to this, Leverstock Green was just the green itself and the wide verge of common grazing land which ran from the green on either side of the Berkhamsted Way, as far as High Street Green. It was also an alias for the small roughly triangular Manor of Market Oak. This stretched from the green to just beyond Blackwater Lane and was bounded by the two principal routeways.

By the time Victoria came to the throne, the small brick and tile making industry had begun to grow, so that by the late 1850s brick making was an important local industry, bringing with it an increase in population and the need for a local church.

Despite the brick industry which continued until the 1930s, Leverstock Green was essentially a rural village community. During the first half of this century some residential development took place, but the biggest changes came with the development of the large residential estates in the 1960s as part of the New Town. A new Village Centre was created, and the green enlarged to it's present size.

The majority of the photographs in this book provide a nostalgic look back at Leverstock Green before the development which began in the 1960s. Interest in our past has never been greater, and I hope these photographs will help open a window onto that past and help us to retain a pride in our local heritage, ensuring that a sense of belonging to the Leverstock Green community continues.

One
Around and About

Leverstock Green c. 1900. The road to St Albans, now known as Leverstock Green Road runs through the village, changing to the Hemel Hempstead Road as it leaves the built-up area. From the Middle Ages until the nineteenth century it was known as the Berkhamsted Way or Berkhamsted Highway.

Leverstock Green, looking SE *c*. 1900. Taken by local pupil teacher Mary Olive Dell, (see photo on page 59) it typifies the peaceful rural village of the early days of this century. The finger post behind the group of children standing in the road, directed the local traveller to Redbourne. Further down the road signs for The Three Horseshoes and The White Horse, welcome the locals and travellers alike. To the right of the Church, the sign outside the Rose and Crown can just be seen. A young boy in the costume typical of the time, is standing outside Hillside Cottages, to the right in the foreground. The width of the grass verges can clearly be seen, with a horse cropping the grass, possibly waiting to be shod at the Blacksmiths. These verges constituted the common grazing land from the Middle Ages in what was predominantly an arable area. Leverstock Green being originally the name of the long strip of common 'green' running all the way from Church Road, to High Street Green.

Waiting to be shod *c.* 1945. These two working farm horses are waiting their turn outside the smithy at the end of Blacksmith's Row. Blacksmiths are known to have worked from these premises since the mid-eighteenth century. The last blacksmith still worked here until the mid-1950s.

Hillside Cottages, postmarked 1954. The inscription on the reverse says: 'This shows the fat little pony and the funny little milk cart that Mr Boatwright used to bring round Leverstock Green.' In those days milk was poured directly from the milkman's jug into his customer's container.

The Village Centre *c*. 1910. Possibly the first motor car to disturb the village's peace can just be made out outside the Post Office. All the buildings to the left of the road were demolished in the 1960s to make way for the present Village Centre.

The Three Horseshoes public house and general store. Tom Perkins and his wife Mary Elizabeth moved here in 1904, when this photo was taken. Tom kept a market garden behind the premises, while his wife ran the grocery store.

12

The Three Horseshoes Grocery and Provision Stores *c.* 1908. By the 1920s the Perkins family were also operating an occasional taxi service.

The Three Horseshoes Garage *c.* 1940. By 1933 the Three Horseshoes had become established as the village garage. There was also a tea room which catered for cycling parties. Today all that remains is the name, which the modern Mobil filling station retained.

Walking to School *c*. 1900. These girls in their pinafores would have been on their way to the village school in the Bedmond Road (see page 58). Today the journey to school is at the height of the rush-hour, with almost nose-to-tail traffic through the village. The figure to be seen walking in the Hemel direction, and between the White Horse, (the building with the white gable end) and The Three Horseshoes, can just be made out to be carrying a wooden yoke around his shoulders, on which would be balanced pales of milk.

The Stump Pond, 1905. Particularly in winter, a large pond was formed on the Green. It was visited by several ducks, and provided entertainment for the village children, who often got rather wet in the course of their games. The Leather Bottle public house is the building with the arch over the door. The shed like building immediately to it's left was the wheelwright's (and undertaker's) workshop.

Playing on The Green *c.* 1900. The long grass of the green in summer made an excellent playground for the village children. With only the occasional horse-drawn wagon passing through, it was very safe.

The Green and Village Centre, June 1945. The road through the village was much narrower than today, and there were no pavements. It is easy to see how fairs and other pastimes took place on the green, even before it was enlarged to its present size.

Village Shop and Post Office c. 1940. Leverstock Green is known to have had a post office as early as 1870, when John Child was the sub-postmaster and parish clerk.

The Post Office and White Horse public house *c*. 1950. The earliest recorded landlord of the White Horse in 1840 was William Cooper, although it had probably served as an ale-house long before then. The building was demolished in the 1960s and the new White Horse public house built back along the road, next to the junction with Green Lane.

Post Office and Stores *c*. 1960. By the end of the 1950s the Post Office and general stores had extended into the whole of the ground floor of the cottages.

The War Memorial *c*. 1920. Erected in the first months of 1919, the memorial originally had no iron railings surrounding it. Plans are currently being discussed to move the memorial to the area of green behind Church Cottages, where a Garden of Remembrance is to be built.

Church Cottages and the War Memorial *c*. 1950. Church Cottages form an island surrounded by green. The road to Bedmond and Watford is to the right and the road to St Albans to the left. Both routes were of Roman origin, and it was the 'waste' which developed where they converged which led to the formation of the original green.

The Church and Pond, 1905. The Rose and Crown public house, on the right of the picture, is now a private house. A modern view from the same spot, would just show the cricket pavilion on the far right of the pond.

Bedmond Road, looking NW *c.* 1950. The back of Church Cottages can be seen on the right. Earlier in the century a pond could be found behind these cottages. Near where the cricket pavilion is today, there used to be a well, used by several of the locals, including the village school.

The Leather Bottle c. 1935. Known to have been licensed premises from at least 1786 when Jeremiah Pope was the licencee, The Leather Bottle has always played an important role in village life.

The Leather Bottle from its garden, late 1940s. The garden has long since disappeared, being replaced with an enclosed car-park. The wooden building behind the car was the wheelwright's shop, run by Robert William Wright. Mr Wright was also the village undertaker and parish clerk.

The Leather Bottle *c.* 1954. The cars parked outside, and the television aerial, are a good indication of how the pace of modern life was increasing in the village. Increased trade had led to a small extension.

Outside the Leather Bottle, 4 September 1958. Waiting outside for a bus were Madge Field (née Parkins) and her young daughter Angela. Madge's parents were the licencees of the pub, having taken over the licence from Madge's grandmother, who had in turn succeeded her husband Arthur Seabrook. Mr Seabrook had taken on the licence in 1883.

Leverstock Green Farm, 1940. This farmhouse dates back to 1644 and possibly earlier. Considerable documentation exists concerning this farm from the seventeenth century onwards. It was known as Carpenter's Farm until the end of the last century, as a Thomas Carpenter purchased the copyhold of the farm in 1671. Until earlier this century, Carpenter's was a working farm of approximately sixty-three acres. Ten acres were on the opposite side of the road, in the manor of Gorhambury, the remaining acres were all in the parish and manor of Abbots Langley. The land was for the most part a furlong wide strip stretching back as far as the present day Leys Road in Bennetts End, and included Hobb Jill (or Hobbs Hill) Wood. The northerly boundary of the farm coinciding with the Hemel Hempstead/Abbots Langley parish boundary, and the southerly boundary, with the exception of seven acres called the Heath, roughly where Hobbs Hill Wood School is today, being Pease Lane. This was an ancient lane which more or less coincided with the present day Peascroft Road. By 1939 the farmhouse had only ten acres of land, and was no longer a working farm.

Leverstock Green Farmhouse, winter 1950. This view was taken from the paddock. Windemere Close was later built on the land which made up the paddock.

Leverstock Green Farmhouse, after renovation, 1964. Considerable restoration work was done on the house and later the barn. (To the right, out of the picture.) The barn is now the offices of CellPath Plc. Note the view across the road, with no modern White Horse pub.

Mafeking and Coronation Villas *c.* 1930. Old Leverstock and The Brairs are set back between them. Without pavements, and with very narrow roads, it can be seen how these Victorian houses, built of local brick, were built 'on the green'.

Mafeking Villas *c.* 1935. Now known as Nos 1 and 2 Greenside, both houses have been extended, particularly the left-hand one, which has a whole bay added to it. The garden , where the trees can be seen, is now the exit road from the Village Centre and car park.

Sibleys Orchard *c*. 1900. The architect of this Victorian house was Norman Stone. It was the home for many years of the Websters, a family of London Goldsmiths. It is now an Abbeyfield Society house, giving a home to several active elderly people. It has recently had a single story extension. The pond is no longer there, although when it rains heavily, water has a tendency to collect at the junction of Chambersbury Lane and the Bedmond Road.

Chambersbury c. 1950. This Georgian facaded house stood back from the Bedmond Road at the head of Chambersbury Lane until the mid 1960s, when it was demolished to make way for modern houses. It is unclear if this house was older than it's appearance, but a manor house stood on this site from the middle ages, probably taking its name originally from the fourteenth-century Chaumbre family. Robert de la Chaumbre was known to live in the area in 1370 and William atte Chaumbre in 1394. Chambersbury was a small manor in it's own right, from which was derived the income for the incumbent of St Lawrence's Church, Abbots Langley, and as such was part of the lands belonging to St Albans Abbey. It was also, therefore, known as Rectory Manor. At the dissolution it was sold by Henry VIII to his embroiderer William Ibgrave. Over the centuries Chambersbury had various distinguished owners including Edward, Lord Bruce of Kinloss; Sir Thomas Fullerton; and the Child family, with whom it became part of the Langleybury estate. It then passed to the Filmer family, and was later sold to John Dickinson. He lent it to his daughter Harriot and her husband John Evans shortly after their marriage. From the 1870s until 1949 it was in the Bailey family. Joseph Bailey the younger being one of the founders of the Boxmoor Ironworks, the agricultural engineers based in Bridge Street Hemel Hempstead, until Joseph Bailey's death in 1949.

The Cherry Orchard, Bedmond Road *c*. 1925. Part of the Chambersbury estate, the orchard was let at harvest time. Seen here are Harry Matthews, Jess Smith and another member of the Matthews family. Whilst the cherries were on the trees, at least one member of the family would live in a small hut in the orchard, to scare away the birds with his rifle (see page 122).

King Charles II Cottage, Westwick Row, 1953. The cottage has since been extended in keeping with its original style and its magnificently kept gardens are usually opened to the public once or twice a year. Probably not built until shortly after 1696, the cottage's name is a misnomer, Charles II dying in 1685.

Kiffs Farm, Westwick Row *c.* 1895. Today the cottage is almost unrecognisable, all the weather boarding having been removed, and the cottage sympathetically renovated. It is known today as Dell Cottage, an appropriate name as members of the Dell family lived here in the mid-sixteenth century. The present cottage is at least 300 years old, although it is uncertain if it is the original cottage on the site. From about 1895 it was the home of the local fishmonger and his family (see page 114). The farms and cottages along and leading from Westwick Row formed the principle settlement in this area from the Middle Ages until the eighteenth century, when more cottages started being built around the green. Westwick is officially classed as a Shrunken Medieval Village, which had originally spread out from Gorhambury. A Great Tithe Barn was situated near the far end of the Row, which was demolished in 1633. The Manor of Westwick was established in Saxon times, and is thought to have had its origins in the villa estate of the Romano-British villa at Gorhambury.

The gravel pit *c.* 1924. Excavation for sand and gravel took place in the old brickfield near The Dells, home of Herbert Secretan, during the 1920s. The site can be clearly seen on the map, (page 6) marked as a small brickfield at the village end of Tile Kiln Lane.

About five or six men were employed in the gravel pit, often working well up to their knees in water (see p.121). During the 1914-18 war, Mr Secretan allowed the area to be used as a miniature firing range for the Queen's Westminster Rifles whilst they were stationed in the village.

Belconey *c.* 1920. Belconey was the name given to a group of cottages along Leverstock Green Road, of which The Plough was one. The car in this picture is travelling towards Cox Pond, with The Plough being behind the photographer. The cottages were demolished and replaced with modern chalet bungalows.

Coxpond *c.* 1916. Looking towards Belconey and Leverstock Green village, Little Coxpond Farm is the whitewashed farmhouse just the other side of the pond. During the Second World War the pond, which was very deep, was used to test amphibious craft.

Great Coxpond Farm *c.* 1925. This photograph was entered by Mary Olive Dell in a village competition. It is thought to have gained third prize. Situated on the other side of the road to the pond pictured on the opposite page, it was farmed by Fred Wells at the time of this photograph. Bought by the Brock family (of firework fame), in about 1932, this wonderful and extremely old farm was demolished to make way for homes for their skilled workers brought from Sutton. The firework factory was at Cupid Green, but the children attended Leverstock Green School where they soon made friends and were assimilated into village life. Some of the farmland behind the new houses was developed into the Greenhills Sports Club. The Greenhills Club was then primarily for Brock's employees, but also became the home for many of Leverstock Green's sporting activities until the development of the New Town. Vauxhall Road and Ranelagh Road were named after the gardens in London where, since the eighteenth century, frequent and spectacular displays of Brock's fireworks were ignited for the entertainment of high society. Arthur Brock is buried in Holy Trinity churchyard.

Cox Pond, mid 1950s. The water-table was dropping, and the pond became clogged with weed. New Town housing, can be seen to the east of the pond. The pond is now completely dried up, but until the summer of 1995 the railings were still to be seen. They were removed when two new mini roundabouts were installed to ease traffic flow at rush hours.

The Crabtree public house c. 1950. Today it has been extended to the right, to accommodate a new restaurant. In the seventeenth century it served as one of the local pest houses, i.e. an early isolation hospital-cum-workhouse. Earlier this century, as well as being a beer house, a bakery was also run from the premises, and the owner sold straw for the straw-plait trade.

Breakspears *c.* 1949. Situated virtually at Junction 8 of the M1, there has been a farmstead on the same site since the very earliest times. The probable remains of a Roman Villa or farmstead were unearthed during the construction of the M1, and it is thought to be linked to the Roman Temple mausoleum nearby at Woodlane End. Documentation relating to a farmstead on the site of the present house, and with the same name, can be traced back to 1359. How it received its name is uncertain as there is no documented evidence of a connection with Nicholas Breakspear, Pope Adrian IV, who was born at Kings Langley and became Pope in 1154.

Breakspears *c.* 1970. Amazingly, despite it's proximity to the motorway, this Grade II listed building is still lived in, protected from the motorway by a screen of 3,000 trees. This house was built in the seventeenth century as part of the general improvements to the Gorhambury estate.

Gipsies near Leverstock Green *c.* 1940. Gipsies frequently used to camp around Leverstock Green. One of the favourite spots for the poorer travellers who only had tents, was Market Oak Dell, off Bedmond Road. Market Oak (or Markyate Oak) was the original name of the Manor of Leverstock Green. It consisted of a not very large, almost triangular stretch of land, which ran from more or less where Church Road is today, to just beyond Blackwater Lane, it's boundaries being the Bedmond Road and the Berkhamsted Way (the road to St Albans.) Other gipsies, including these, camped near to where Green Lane meets Buncefield Lane and Westwick Row. It was a favourite spot, as was the area around the reservoir (now the water tower) off Blackwater Lane.

Two

Church and Chapel

Holy Trinity Church Leverstock Green *c.* 1900. The graves look somewhat macabre raised above the ground.

CHURCH OF THE HOLY TRINITY, LEVERSTOCK

GREEN, NEAR ST. ALBAN'S, HERTS.

THIS Church was consecrated on the 30th October, by the Lord Bishop of Rochester. Its erection originated in the munificence of the Earl of Verulam, who presented the site, and a large sum towards the cost of the building.

The edifice is constructed in a substantial manner, and consists of a well-designed chancel, with vestry on the north side; a nave, north and south aisles,

NEW CHURCH AT LEVERSTOCK-GREEN.

and south porch. The bells are hung in a double bell cot, at the west end. The style of the architecture is of the early part of the fourteenth century. The body of the church affords accommodation for four hundred persons in open benches; but at least six hundred were present on the day of consecration. After this impressive ceremony, the service of the day was performed by the Rev. Mr. Hutchinson; and an excellent sermon was delivered by the Hon. and Rev. Edward H. Grimston. The design of the Church, which has given universal satisfaction, was prepared, more than three years since, by Messrs. Raphael and J. Arthur Brandon, and has been carried out by the elder after the lamented decease of his brother.

Adjoining the Church is the Rectory-house, also built from the design, and under the superintendence of the same architect: it is a commodious and appropriate structure.

Extract from *The Illustrated London News*, 10 November 1849.

Holy Trinity Church, 1905. The flu pipe which can be seen above the porch was from the flanged Gurney stove which stood at the west end of the church and provided the only heating until 1939 when central heating was installed.

The Vicarage, Pancake Lane *c.* 1900. By the late 1940s this had become a private residence (Danehurst), and the present rectory had been built. Danehurst was demolished in 1985 to make way for modern housing (Trinity Mews). In Victorian times the Annual Feast Day of the Day and Sunday School was held in its grounds, and this century it was the scene of many pageants, fetes and other village activities.

The Revd Robert Helme, 1861-1871. The Revd Helme changed his name to Mashiter soon after he left the Parish. Behind the font is a window dedicated to five of his children, baptised in the font between 1862 and 1867. A plaque on the wall under the baptistry was erected to the Revd Mashiter after his death in 1909, aged 79.

Interior of Leverstock Green Church c. 1900. Note the oil lamps which provided light in the church until electricity was installed in 1939. Electric light was a gift from the the Brock family in memory of the late Arthur Brock. The wrought iron brackets still remain.

The Revd George Finch, 1871-1899. The Revd Finch died in office at the age of 63, and was buried in Holy Trinity Churchyard on 28 June 1899. He was probably a member of the Finch family from Corner Farm at the junction of Westwick Row and the Hemel Hempstead Road. Members of the Finch (or Fynche) family were yeoman farmers in Westwick from the sixteenth century.

Holy Trinity *c.* 1920. The church clock was installed by public subscription in 1878. It has recently been wired for electrical power. The church hall, known as the Trinity Room, was not added to the west end of the church until 1974.

Holy Trinity from the Bedmond Road *c.* 1935. The conifers in front of the church have grown considerably since the photographs shown earlier.

Left: The Revd Arthur Durrant, 1899-1936. Right: The Revd T. Alexander Binns, 1936-1938.

The East End of the Church, 1943. The high altar, a single slab of stone on six oak legs, had been part of the refurbishment of the east end by the Revd Durrant in 1932, as a memorial to his family. This had taken the form of a huge carved oak screen and carved oak presbyter stalls designed by Sir Walter Tapper, as well as the new altar. The four gilded angels, carved from mahogany by Miss Brenda Bessant who had lived at Tile Kiln House, were presented by the congregation in 1942 in memory of the Revd Arthur Durrant who died in office in 1936. The Revd Durrant's funeral service took place on Wednesday 8 July 1936 after a requiem mass in the morning. He was buried alongside his wife Alice Mabel Durrant, and his youngest daughter Dorothy Mary Clayton East Clayton, widow of Sir Robert Clayton East Clayton. An explorer and pioneer aviator, Dorothy had been tragically killed in an aircraft accident at Brooklands in 1933.

Left: The Revd Richard A. Yates, 1939-1946. Right: The Revd Philip E. Thomas, 1947-1953.

The East End, Holy Trinity, 1949. Erected in 1932, the screen cut the church in two. In 1985 the screen was moved back to the sanctuary step, thus creating a new Lady Chapel behind it. Other work was undertaken at the same time, and the original oak of the stalls reworked to form sedelia in the new sanctuary which was also enlarged.

Vicar's presentation, 1948. At a ball held in their honour, the Revd Philip Thomas and his wife were presented with a cheque and a garden hose by Madge Parkins and Alice Lawrence, to commemorate the completion of their first year at Leverstock Green. The cake was presented by Jean Aldridge for their son Alan. George Mason and his band provided the music (see page 92).

Holy Trinity's centenary concert, Wednesday 26 October 1949. Held in the church, the Leverstock Green Choral Group provided the principal items, conducted by Mr Leslie Regan. The soloist in Mozart's *D Major Violin Concerto* was Mr Sydney Humphreys right of centre (see photograph on page 45).

The Webster Chalice components.

The Webster Chalice. Many gifts, including a total of £208 from the congregation for redecorating the church, were given to the church to celebrate its centenary. One of the principal individual gifts was this hand-made silver-gilt chalice. Made by Malcolm Webster, the chalice was presented by Malcolm, Bernard and Isobel Webster in memory of their late father Percy Webster of Sibleys Orchard. The top picture shows the component parts of the chalice, before being 'water-gilded' and fixed together.

Festival of Britain Concert, 1951. A concert of choral and orchestral music to celebrate the Festival of Britain, featured the Leverstock Green Choral Group. Held at Holy Trinity Church at 8pm on Thursday 18 October, the conductor was Leslie Regan. Taking part in the concert were; sopranos: Barbara Aldous, Eileen Anthony, Ann Gimson, Madge Parkins, Olive Reay, Kathleen Smith. Contraltos: Ethel Brooks, Grace Butler, Dorothy Hart, Vera Presland, Annie Webster. Tenors: John Brooks, Albert Bruce, Reggie Childs, William Griffin, James Rowe, Charles Rowe. Basses: Allen Engles, Bernard Field, Ronald Reay, Harry Squibb, and Philip Thomas. The vicar's wife, Marjorie Thomas (in the centre of the picture in a white satin blouse) played the piano. Norah Regan, William Read, Raymond Ovens and Mary Leaf played the violins; Geoffrey Gotch and Diana Drewer the violas; Susanna Thomas and Ivan Cane the cellos. Sydney Humphreys was violin soloist.

Blessing of St Faith's garage chapel, 6 October 1951. The Bishop of St Albans blessed the garage at No. 4 Windmill Road (Adeyfield) which was to serve as a chapel for the new residents of Adeyfield. The garage was at the home of the Revd Peter Stokes who had been appointed priest-in-charge at Adeyfield. The church itself wasn't completed until 1953, and was, until the formation of the team parish of Hemel Hempstead, within the parish of Leverstock Green. It was, however, intended originally that Adeyfield should be made into a parish in its own right. Members of Holy Trinity choir and congregation attended the ceremony. The Revd Thomas can be seen (just behind the line post) with the Revd Stokes in the procession of the clergy. Bernard Field from Holy Trinity, was carrying the Cross (to the right of the Bishop).

The Garage Chapel. The Revd Peter Stokes conducting a service in the garage chapel. Soon, however, it proved to be far too small and it also suffered from condensation.

Sunday School in The Longland's Hut. Having become impractical in the garage chapel, church services and other activities took place in a contractor's hut off Longlands, before the completion of the new church of St Barnabus.

The newly finished church of St Barnabus, 1953, was still officially a daughter church of Holy Trinity, Leverstock Green.

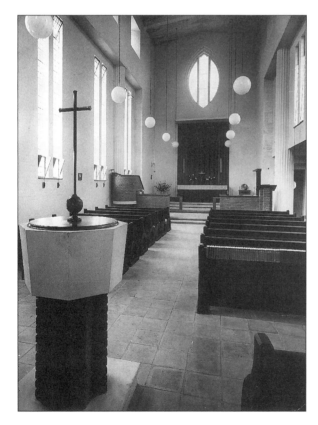

Interior of St Barnabus' church, 1953. The interior was damaged by fire in May 1991. The repairs included a new ceiling, roof and interior decoration.

Holy Trinity sunday school *c.* 1920. This photograph was taken outside the village school in Bedmond Road, where the sunday school was held. Seated in the centre of the picture is the Revd Durrant, to his left as we view the photo is Olive Seabrook. At the far left of that row is Millie Fanmer, née Currell. Seated to the right of the Revd Durrant was his wife and then Sybil Seabrook. Others in the photograph included Lorna Durrant, Violet, Dolly, Sally, Jim and Alf Steers, Florrie and Charlie Latchford, Irene and Gladys DeBeger, Marjorie Bigginshaw and Mrs Bedwell. The village school, which was a Church of England foundation, always had a very close association with the church and the incumbent of the day. The early school log books record almost daily visits by the clergy and frequent visits by the older children to attend a mid-week Divine Service.

'Mission Impossible' children's mission, 1969. Held in a marquee on Leverstock Green playing fields for a week in 1969, the mission was led by Evangelist Gordon Pettie (on stage), assisted by members of Holy Trinity including Joan Sweeney and Audrey Baillie (centre back).

Outside the mission marquee. Tony Andrews (with glasses) can be seen coming out of the marquee. The mission attracted many children from around the area, not just Sunday School members. Parents attended the final gathering.

Sunday school annual picnic in the late 1960s. Mary Clarke is dispensing liquid refreshment to some of the members of Holy Trinity Sunday School at their annual summer picnic held in the grounds of her home, Breakspears.

Exploring Breakspears. Members of the sunday school, led by Sarah Beacon, explore the gounds of Breakspears as part of their picnic fun.

One of the first Good Friday workshops *c.* 1970. Holy Trinity's Good Friday workshops are open to all village children and are still held every year. Seen here are, left to right: Michelle Goman, Dianne Millis, Debbie Geary and Jane Denslow.

Supervising the Good Friday workshop, *c.* 1970, are left to right: Audrey Baillie, Ann Clarke and Linda Rayner.

Recorder group at the Good Friday workshop. *c*. 1970. From left to right: Julie Dell, Dianne Millis, Karen Gillon, Debbie Geary and Michelle Goman.

Music group at Good Friday workshop *c*. 1970. These photos were taken at the school in Pancake Lane. Since the amalgamation of the two schools in the village, the workshops now meet at the school in Green Lane.

Carol singing on the Green, December 1973. Members of Holy Trinity Church have regularly gone round the village at Christmas time singing carols to raise money for charity. Note the newly built village hall to the rear of the pub. The hall didn't officially open until July the following year.

Still singing carols, December 1973. The Revd John Morris can be seen on the right of the picture, in front of the bus. A group of children playing recorders helped to keep everyone in tune.

The Baptist chapel *c.* 1900. Built in 1841, the Baptist chapel preceded the church by eight years and always had a thriving congregation. When no longer required as a chapel, it was used as a welfare clinic. By 1969 it had been demolished and a private house, No. 18 Bedmond Road, built on the site.

Baptist chapel outing to Kent, late 1930s. From the mid-nineteenth century the members of the Baptist congregation had an annual outing or treat. Some of those here are: Mrs Rogers, Mrs G. Matthews, Mrs W. Matthews, Lily Wilkins, Mrs Seeby, Mrs Childs, Mrs Wilkins, Mrs Mayo, and Hilda Lavender.

Demolition of Roman Catholic church, 1985. The Roman Catholic Church of St Mary the Virgin, built between the new dual-carriageway (St Albans Road) and Ritcroft Street in 1958, unfortunately suffered from structural problems and had to be rebuilt.

Interior during demolition, 1985. After considerable wrangling over who should foot the bill, the church was eventually demolished, and a new church, Our Lady Queen of All Creation, built on the same site.

Three
The Happiest Days of Their Lives

Pupils at Leverstock Green school *c.* 1890. This picture was taken against the walls of the school which was in Bedmond Road.

The Schools, Bedmond Road *c*. 1900. In about 1840, a Dame school built by public subscription was opened in the Old School House (which still stands today). As the numbers of children attending the school increased, it became obvious that a larger school was needed, and in 1846, out of the private purse of the curate of Abbots Langley (in whose parish this was), a school was built adjoining the Old School House. It had a room which could be divided into two sections by a curtain. As it was a few years before Holy Trinity church was built, Divine services were held in the school on Sundays. The school was extended in 1857 and 1887 and was eventually abandoned in 1931 for a new site in Pancake Lane. The then headmaster, Walter Ayre, continued to live in the Old School House, which is still inhabited by his daughter. The rest of the school buildings were eventually demolished and modern houses built in their stead.

Headmaster Thomas Henry Ford and pupils *c*. 1897. Also in the picture are his wife, Mrs Olivia Ford, who was the Infant Mistress, and two pupil teachers. Mr Ford was the first headmaster to be appointed to Leverstock Green school, and served in that post from 1888-1919. This photograph is believed to have been taken in 1897. The pupil teacher kneeling in front of Mr Ford is Mary Olive Dell. Born in the village in 1880 she moved away to teach elsewhere, but eventually returned to live with her mother and sister Beryl in Pancake Lane. Know as the Miss Dells of Pancake Lane, they were very active members of the local community and Mary Olive was a keen amateur photographer. Several of the photographs used throughout this book were taken by her.

School group c. 1898. If you study the two pictures on this page, you will see that many of the same faces can be seen.

School group c. 1899.

Mr Ford and pupils c. 1910. It is interesting to note that the picture was taken by the Scholastic Souvenir Co. of Bispham, Blackpool. The annual school photograph is obviously a well-established tradition.

Boys From Leverstock Green School c. 1914. Most of the boys had obviously done their best to dress as smartly as possible with their breeches and Norfolk Jackets. The fashion in boots has gone full circle with the modern trend for 'Doc Martens'.

Boys from Leverstock Green school, *c.* 1914. It is interesting to note that some of the boys had obviously borrowed hats or caps and that a few were wearing the sailor suits popularised in the previous century by Queen Victoria's family.

Thomas Ford and pupils *c.* 1918. Back row, left to right: C. Wilkins, C. Latchford, R. Sears, F. Bridges, Arthur Clark, A. Ray, E. Major. Front row: J. Shapcott, L.Rance, I. De Begar, S. Steers, R. Thorne, F. Shapcott, E. Packham. Crossed legged: F. Hoar, A. Brown.

Miss Herbert and pupils, c. 1923. Back row, left to right are: Raymond Dell, Bill King, Fred Douse, Miss Herbert, Bob Biswell, Bill Gale. In the bottom row are: George Foulder, Henry Briggs, Jim Blackie, Alf Steers, Bill Matthews, Les Perry and Don Field.

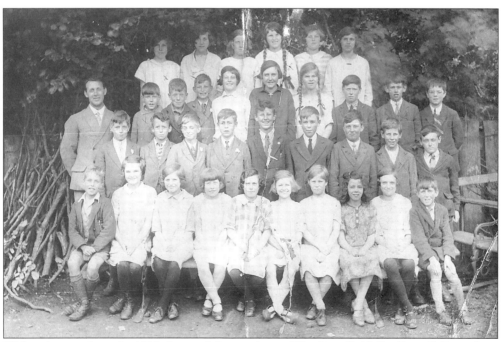

Walter Ayre and pupils, 1928. Some of the pupils are: Win Biswell, Nellie Biswell, Doris Cox, Vera Windsor, Jim Matthews, Gil Steers, David Shapcott, Olive Foulder, Win Wilkins, Dimp Cox, Herbert Wheeler, Len Baleter, Bob Shapcott, Reg Childs, Don Field, Ron West, Syd Ison, Cecil King, Jack Gala, Mavis Seabrook, Dorris Pedder, Audrey Wilson, Kitty Field, May Matthews, Olive Godman, Amy Persil and Bob Perry.

The march to Pancake Lane, 11 October 1930. By 1930 the school in Bedmond Road had got into such a state of disrepair that it was condemned by the Education Department. The number of pupils had increased and a new school became necessary. The Earl of Verulam gave the site of Bluebell Wood in Pancake Lane, and a great deal of fundraising took place to help pay for the school buildings. It was a true village effort and involved everyone within the community. The vicar, The Revd Durrant, was frequently seen around the village with his collecting bag. Marmalade, jam, cakes and handicrafts were made and sold. It was frequently said that the school was built on marmalade! Eventually in October, the village children processed down Pancake Lane to see the foundation stone laid and blessed.

Blessing the new school, 11 October 1930. The entire village turned out to see the Bishop lay the foundation stone and bless the site of the new school, which was eventually to be used for the first time on 20 April 1931, and officially opened a month later on 2 May. The stone commemorating the event was transferred to the present school in Green Lane when the school in Pancake Lane was in it's turn closed in 1985. There is, however, still a village school, as Leverstock Green Church of England Primary School and Westwick JMI merged to form Leverstock Green JMI (C. of E. controlled). The inscription on the stone is, however, inaccurate, as the Bishop of St Albans was actually officiating at the memorial service for victims of the R101 airship disaster at Cardington. His place in Leverstock Green was taken by the Bishop Suffragan of Bedford.

Walter Ayre and pupils, outside the new school. *c.* 1933. Surrounded by woods, the children were able to watch small woodland creatures come up to the french doors of their classroom. The relatively large airy and well lit rooms were a far cry from the old school in Bedmond Road.

In the playground at Pancake Lane, *c.* 1947. Included in the photo are, front row: Jean Faithful (left). Seated: Margaret Lumb and Jill Parkins. Boys: Derek Greenfield, Eric Gurney, Joseph Chamberlain, Norman Ivory, James Dunbar, Godfrey Foulder and James Dawkins.

Leverstock Green school 'Market Stalls', 1963. Children from the primary school in Pancake Lane admire their handiwork.

Watching a play in the hall at Pancake Lane *c.* 1963.

Westwick school children on a visit to the fire station, October 1969. With the expansion of the New Town development, an additional school in the village became necessary. In 1962 a new primary school, called Westwick School, was opened in Green Lane. It eventually merged with the school in Pancake Lane, on the Green Lane site, in 1985.

Leverstock Green Scouts *c*. 1908. This is thought to have been taken in the vicarage gardens and shows on the back row, left to right: Percy Dell, Will Steer, -?-, Cecil Parkins. Front row: Fred Harrowell, Victor Perkins, V. Walt and Bernard Wright. Several of these boys died during the 1914-18 war.

Leverstock Green Girl Guides *c*. 1914. At the centre of the group of guides is the Revd Durrant. The large straw boaters were then an essential part of the uniform, replaced later by felt hats and eventually by the more modern stewardess style hats. The triangular bandage style tie enabled the females of the Scout movement to be as 'prepared' as their male counterparts.

Leverstock Green Girl Guides *c*. 1936. These guides were more relaxed than the previous generation. Notice the difference in head gear, where they are wearing anything at all. The dresses, or skirts and blouses were blue, with pale blue ties. The present uniform, designed by Geoff Banks, is more casual, with blue sweatshirts and dark blue sashes.

Brownies from the 1st Leverstock Green Troop *c.* 1956. Until the 1980s the Brownie's uniform was very similar to that of the Guides, only in brown (with a yellow tie), rather than in blue. Brown woolly hats were introduced to replace the berets but now the entire uniform is more casual with yellow sweatshirts and brown sashes.

Preparing the ground for Leverstock Green's Scout headquarters, September 1969. Hemel Hempstead's Mayor, John Doyle, cut the first sod of the new Leverstock Green Scout Headquarters in Pancake Lane. Compare these Scouts' uniforms with those of sixty years earlier (page 68).

Four
Bennetts End

Woodside, Bennetts End *c.* 1905. This property was off Tile Kiln Lane, approximately where the end of Marston Close is today. In Kelley's Directory of 1933 it was listed as being the commercial residence of George Bailey, farmer. He was a brother of Joseph Bailey of Chambersbury.

Tile Kiln Lane *c.* 1905. This was very much a country lane, speed humps were unnecessary! The central property is the half-timbered sixteenth-century cottage known today as The Old Cottage. The brick works was behind the cottages in the picture. The other cottages were built for brick workers sometime in the eighteenth century and are still standing.

Orchard Lea, Tile Kiln Lane *c.* 1905. Further back than the present numbers 23 and 25, all that is left of this property is the remains of the garden wall, built out of local brick. At differing times it was known as Bennetts End House and Bennetts End Lodge. Bonamy Panmore Eykyn, the owner at the time of this postcard, can be seen with his family on the lawn.

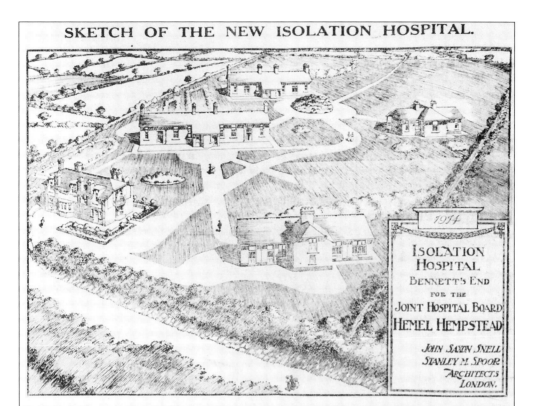

SKETCH OF THE NEW ISOLATION HOSPITAL.

1914

ISOLATION
HOSPITAL
BENNETT'S END
FOR THE
JOINT HOSPITAL BOARD
HEMEL HEMPSTEAD

JOHN SAXON SNELL
STANLEY M. SPOOR
ARCHITECTS
LONDON.

This building for which a contract was entered into by the Hemel Hempstead Joint Hospital Board on June 30th, comprises the following accommodation: 22 beds for patients, including 12 beds for scarlet fever, 5 beds for diphtheria, and 2 beds for observation cases, staff accommodation for non-resident medical officer, matron, five nurses, and two servants, and the usual establishment kitchen, offices, etc, a hand power laundry, steam disinfector, mortuary and ambulance house, stores, etc. The buildings are to be carried out with brindled red facing bricks of local manufacture, and the roofs covered with red tiles. A paved area is also provided for the reception of tents in case of emergency.

The amount of the accepted tender £5,989, or under £275 per bed.

The architects are Messrs. John Saxon Snell and Stanley M. Spoor, of London. The quantities being by Mr. Alfred R. Evans, of London, and the builders are Messrs. C Miskin and Sons, Ltd., of St. Albans.

The *Gazette*'s feature on the New Isolation Hospital, 18 July 1914.

Belswains Farm *c.* 1950. Looking NE, from what is now Belswains Lane, the wooded area to the right on the horizon is Hobbs Hill Wood (opposite the present school). The wooded area to the left on the horizon is where, at one time, there were lime kilns. On what became Jarmans Field is now Leisure World. This farm land is now virtually all covered by housing, built as part of the New Town Development.

Hobbs Hill Wood schools, 26 March 1954. Just completed, as part of the New Town Development, the junior school is in the foreground with the infants school immediately behind the oak tree. The schools were built on what had been, until this development, part of a seven acre field called The Heath. This had belonged to Carpenters Farm (Leverstock Green Farm) from the early seventeenth century. The line of trees in the foreground followed the line of the ancient Pease Lane and was to become Peasecroft Road. The wood, from which the school takes its name, is just out of the bottom right of the picture. The hedges and field boundaries which show up so well, date back to the early Middle Ages, and probably earlier, being Medieval furlong field boundaries. A recent survey of the remaining hedge along the top end of Chambersbury Lane, the boundary which runs diagonally across the top of the picture, dated the hedge to the tenth century.

Children's Christmas party c. 1954. As one of the first neighbourhood areas to be constructed, the inhabitants of the new homes in Bennetts End tended to be employed together in the new factories on the industrial estate. This party, held for the employee's families, was mostly made up of children from the Bennetts End area.

Barnacres residents outing, 1962. Outings to the sea and other places of interest were arranged by various groups of local residents. This trip in 1962 was for the residents of Barnacres.

Hobbs Hill Wood Junior School netball team, 1963-4. Included in the team were Janet Baker, Sally Digby and Marion Perrott.

Hobbs Hill Wood Junior School sports day, July 1963. The guest of honour, the Infant School headmistress Miss Morgan, presents the House Shield to the captain of the winning house, Susan Gray. Headmaster Mr Crawford (right), looks on.

Hobbs Hill Wood Junior School summer fair fancy dress, *c.* 1965. Held indoors because of the rain, Mr Crawford is welcoming the infant entrants. Looking on is Ron Bryant (to the right with his arms folded), the chairman of the parents' association.

Fancy dress parade at Hobbs Hill Wood Junior school's summer fair *c.* 1979. To the right of the contestants is Jayne Hardwick with her small brother and sister.

Hobbs Hill Wood Junior School football team, May 1975.

An honorary Brownie, 1982. District Commissioner, Margaret Cox, is seen here presenting Mr Graham Crawford, Headmaster of Hobbs Hill Wood Junior School, with a 'Thankyou Badge'. Seated to their right is Brown Owl, Margaret D. Cox. Some of the Brownies are Jayne Hardwick, Michelle Allen, Christine Russell, Charlotte Cook, Anna Cook, Michelle Powell and Melanie Huggins. Margaret Cox is known to many local children as 'Aunty Margaret' of the Roundabout Playgroup which she ran from 1970 until Easter 1996.

Five

In Time of War

Troops Through Leverstock Green *c*. 1914. It is uncertain whether these were the Queen's Westminster Rifles or some of the many other troops to be garrisoned around Hemel Hempstead at the start of the First World War. Here, the troops can be seen passing The Three Horseshoes public house.

F Company, Queens Westminster Rifles, September 1914. The sixteenth Battalion of the 2nd London Division of the Territorial Army, The Queen's Westminster Rifles, arrived in Leverstock Green on 17 August 1914, after a two day march from Hyde Park. F Company were billeted at Leverstock Green Farm, the home of Mr and Mrs John Knox Hart, thought to be the civilians in the picture. Other companies were billeted at Bunkers Farm, Westwick Hall Farm, Well Farm, Corner Farm and Westwick Row Farm, as well as at Westridge and Potters Crouch. The troops remained in Leverstock Green until 1 November when they left for France. Major J.Q. Henriques, who at the time of their billeting in Leverstock Green was the Captain commanding C Company, said in his diary: ' Time at Leverstock Green passed happily and rapidly, the days were fully occupied, the weather was uniformly fine, and the health of the troops was excellent. The kindness and hospitality shown by the local residents was unstinting and will never be forgotten, and it is hoped that they knew how deeply their actions were appreciated.'

Queen's Westminster Rifles billeting party, August 1914 . The group seen here were photographed outside the school in Bedmond Road. The school was set up as their headquarters and used as an orderly room and stores. When school resumed after the harvest holiday, the children had their lessons in the Baptist chapel instead.

Outside Bunkers Farm, September 1914. Members of B Company take their ease. The men quickly made friends in the village, particularly with the young ladies. They left behind them both group and individual photographs as mementos of their stay.

Members of the Hertfordshire Regiment 1914. Many local men joined up, some joining the QWR and several joined the Hertfordshire Regiment, including the three pictured here. Tom Parkins is in the centre, Fred Harrowell is possibly the private on the right. The identity of the private on the left is not known, but he was a member of the 1907 football team.

Walter Parkins c. 1914.

Cecil Parkins *c.* 1914. Son of the village fishmonger, Cecil Parkins was apprenticed to the wheelwright, whose workshop was next to The Leather Bottle. He later married Olive Seabrook, daughter of the landlord of The Leather Bottle and was eventually to become the licensee himself.

Artillery at Well Farm, (Bedmond Road), 1916. Taken from a cutting of *The Watford Journal* for 1 February 1916, this picture shows the kind of troop manoeuvres which were common around the area during the First World War.

Unveiling the War Memorial, 5 February 1919. A sad, but important day in the history of the village, the service of remembrance was attended by virtually the whole village who gathered around the green for the occasion. The Memorial commemorated the lives of twenty-eight members of the Leverstock Green community who had died serving their country. They were: T. Alderman, H. Biswell, G. Brown, F. Charge, A. Chisman, T. Childs, G. De Beger, A.M. Durrant, H. Freeman, F. Freeman, G. Goodenough, J. Hallett, F. Harrowell, J. Knox Hart, F. Johnson, B. Oakley, W. Parkins, V. Perkins, W. W. Sears, R. H. Secretan, H. Smith, F. Taylor, E. Thorn, G. Timson, W. Webb, H. Woodwards, H. Waubruell and B. Wright.

ARP wardens from Leverstock Green, 1940. During the Second World War, many members of the Leverstock Green Community volunteered as ARP wardens. This photograph includes the Leverstock Green contingent.

Drilling the Home Guard, 1941. Seen here in uniform is Corporal Arthur White putting some members of Leverstock Green's Home Guard through their paces. To the left of Corporal White is Bert Lavender and to the right Dougie Fountain and Joe Catlin. It is not known who the rest of the men are.

Some of The Leverstock Green Home Guard *c*. 1942. Their official title was, No.3 Platoon, 'B' Co. of the 9th Hertfordshire Battalion, Home Guard. Originally part of the 5th Herts Battalion, the men of this platoon were drawn from Pimlico and Bedmond, as well as Leverstock Green, and were transferred into the 9th Battalion in April 1942. The platoon numbered over seventy men in total, and was responsible for the largest area in the company, i.e. 5,760 acres. The platoon was eventually divided in December 1943, and a new platoon set up for Bedmond. In command of the platoon was Lieutenant R.A. Shuffrey of Leverstock Green Farm (centre, with his dog, Rags). Pictured are, very back row, left to right: Bob Ison(glasses), -?-, Fred Latchford, -?-, -?-, Tommy Daniels. Centre row: Mrs Guise (woman auxiliary), Bob Fitzjohn, Bert Boatwright, Tom Waller, Jim Stewart, ? Wheeler, Tony Shuffrey, -?-, Cecil Parkins, Dick Sears and Beatie Mayo (woman auxiliary). Front row: Charlie Rogers, Fred Jacques, -?-, -?-, Syd Ison, Bill Skeggs, Lt. R.A. Shuffrey, R. Mann, Edie Perkins, Albert Daniels, -?-. The -?-s include: Arthur White, Bill Lavendar, Doug Fountain, and Joe Catlin.

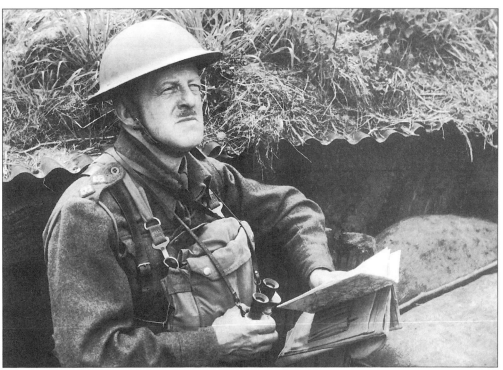

Lt. R. Allen Shuffrey, Commander of the Leverstock Green Home Guard. Lt.Shuffrey is seen here taking part in a field exercise.

The Home Guard's ammunitions dump *c.* 1942, was to be found in the paddock at Leverstock Green Farm.

Brothers Archie (left) and William Foulder (right) were two of the relatively few Leverstock Green casualties of the Second World War.

The War Memorial, late 1940s. Fortunately, relatively few men from the village were killed during the Second World War whilst serving in the forces. Those named on the memorial are: Harry Bagshaw, Gordon Clear, Frank Cokes, Arthur Collins, F. Cother, George Faulder, Archie Faulder, Jack Newland, and James Rogers.

Six

High Days and Holidays

Maypole dancing *c.* 1910. The first of May was always a traditional day of celebration, even when not an official holiday. School attendance was affected as this extract shows: '1 May 1872; Rather a poor school – children kept away to go Maying'. The Baptist chapel is in the background.

Leverstock Green villagers attend Nash Mills outing, 1915. Many members of the Leverstock Green community worked at Dickinsons' Nash Mills, and can be seen here dressed up for their annual outing in 1915. This despite the fact that the country was at war. Note the large buttonholes worn by nearly everyone.

Empire Day, 24 May c. 1930. A service was held around the War Memorial and then the school children were given some sweets and allowed to go home for the rest of the day. The teacher in the centre of the group is Miss Herbert, who used to cycle from Boxmoor everyday, in all weathers.

The Hertfordshire Hunt c. 1937. The hunt regularly met outside the Leather Bottle for their stirrup cup prior to setting off over the fields in search of a fox. Many of the villagers, especially the children, would come out to watch the hunt go off, and make a fuss of the hounds.

A function in the Parish Hall c. 1940. Included are: Violet Hagger, Reg Matthews, Sid Lawrence, Alice White, May Hagger, Win Bisswell, Mrs Rance, Peg Daniels, Mrs Matthews, Margaret Dell, Mrs Fathill, Mrs Daniels, Jim Matthews, Mrs Hagger, Mrs G. Shuffrey, Mrs Perkins, Bernard Field, Mr and Mrs Leek, Edna Dell, and Rita Powell.

Fancy dress ball, 1948. About 200 people attended the ball held at the parish hall in honour of the vicar, the Revd Philip Thomas and his wife. The ball was a spontaneous effort on behalf of the village to commemorate the completion of his first year as vicar. He and his wife were the guests of honour and during the evening were presented with gifts (see page 43). Mrs Helen Guise had coordinated the activities and a great number of people in the village contributed to the arrangements and the expenses. The highlight of the ball was the fancy dress parade. Instructions for dressing up were 'Try and be something connected with gardening.' Mr A.L. Shuffrey won first prize as a scarecrow and his wife Margaret won second prize as a flower seller. The children's prizes were awarded to Ann Reed and Alan Wilson who were a wasp and a bee, respectively. Four competitors turned up with wings announcing they were 'fairies from the bottom of the garden'. Tony Suards was the MC and music was provided by George Mason and his band.

Morris dancing outside the Leather Bottle, 7 June 1952, once a regular sight in the village. Leverstock Green residents would watch and then join in the country dancing afterwards.

Dressed for the Queen, 20 July 1952. After laying the foundation stone for St Barnabus' church, Adeyfield, it was arranged that the Queen should change cars in Leverstock Green prior to being driven to St Albans for a service in the Abbey. This caused considerable excitement in the village, which was royally decorated for the occasion.

Waiting for the Queen. Included in this crowd are Mrs Faulder, Mrs Matthews, Mrs G.I. Shuffrey, Mr Ayre (Special P.C.), Mrs Gwen Matthews, Mrs Freda Matthews, Mrs Mears (in wheel chair), Miss Hobbs, Mrs W. Matthews, Mrs Daniels and Mrs Williamson.

Flag poles outside the White Horse. Several days beforehand flag poles had been erected in the village to fly the Union Flags.

Virtually the whole population of the village, together with their families and friends waited for a chance to glimpse and cheer the young Queen. Many of the people who lined the Green brought boxes and crates to stand on so they could see above other people's heads.

The Royal car. The Queen and the Duke of Edinburgh arrived at 4.45pm, stopping opposite the bus shelter for about one minute only. Not everyone was as fortunate with their snaps as this photographer, most only managing to capture the car's headlights or someone else's hat on film!

Children's fancy dress parade *c*. 1950. The annual village fete has always included a children's fancy dress parade and for many years, as here, the facilities at Brock's Sports Ground (the Greenhills Club, Vauxhall Road) were used.

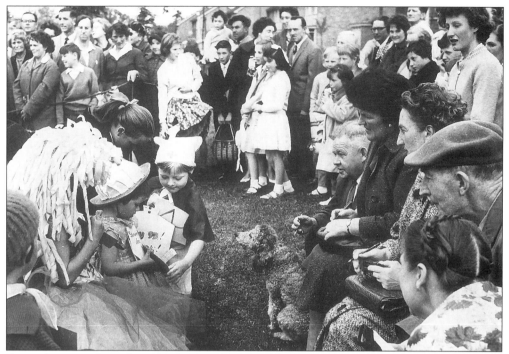

Fancy dress parade, Whit Monday 1962. Yet another fancy dress competition at the annual village fete. Judging the competition (on the right) were Mrs G.D. Marshall, Mr and Mrs Reynolds and Mrs and Miss Featherstone. The competition was followed by a procession, led by folk dancers, from the green to the school in Pancake Lane.

The mayor attends a village function, 1969. Pictured here in the Parish Hall are Mayor John Doyle and his wife together with Mrs Weston, Alice Sears, Mrs Matthews, Mrs Rogers and Mrs Wilkins. The nature of the occasion is not known.

Village wedding *c*. 1905. Weddings have always been an important highlight of village life. Father of the bride is William Parkins, (in the top hat), the bride, Ellen, (his daughter by his first marriage); her groom, William Read; the bride's sister (left) Annie and their two brothers (seated) Will and Thomas. William's second wife Lydia is seated with their youngest son Henry and her three elder sons Frederick, Cecil and Walter, on the grass.

Mr and Mrs Jim Jordan *c*. 1917. In contrast to her sister's wedding, the wedding finery here, with the men in uniform, is quite different. Seated on the rug is Winifred Read. Front row, left to right: Fred Parkins, Ellen Read, Jim Jordan, Annie Parkins, -?-, Lydia Parkins. The back row includes: William Read (left), Walter Parkins (centre, uniform) and Tom Parkins (right), with his wife Emily to his right.

Bridesmaids outside Holy Trinity church *c.* 1928. These young ladies attended Sybil Seabrook at her wedding to Eddie Perkins. The smallest bridesmaid is Madge Parkins, the bride's niece. Fashions had been changing yet again with shorter, drop-waisted skirts and cloche hats.

The wedding of Leslie Seabrook and Lily Wilkins, 1929. Arthur Seabrook, (second left of the front row) was licensee of the Leather Bottle from 1883. He had three children by his second marriage, the youngest being Leslie. His second wife Lily, (née Dell), is seated to his left. Between them is their granddaughter Madge.

Wedding of Kitty Field and William Beaumont, 18 April 1945. Despite still being war time with clothes rationing, this photograph reflects another change in the fashions of the day. As well as the style of the dresses, the ladies' hair styles and head dresses are typical of the 1940s. The cut of the men's uniforms and suits has also changed over the years.

The marriage of Carolyn Baillie and David Martin, 14 April 1979. Seen outside with the happy couple is the Revd John Morris. He was vicar, and then Team Rector at Leverstock Green from 1967 until 1982. Bridal fashions no longer truly reflected everyday wear.

Seven

Pageants, Plays and Pastimes

A pageant in the vicarage gardens *c.* 1925. Pageants played a large part in village life earlier this century, and were usually held in the grounds of the vicarage, with most of the village children and many others taking part.

Scenes from the village pageant in *c*. 1925. This particular pageant was possibly connected with the early christian martyrs and was apparently set during Roman times requiring most of the children to act as slaves.

Beryl Dell *c.* 1925. Beryl Dell lived in Pancake Lane with her mother and sister. Originally apprenticed to a draper in Hemel Hempstead, she became the village dressmaker. She was therefore probably responsible for her own and many of the other costumes for the pageant depicted on the previous two pages. Members of the Dell family have lived in the area since the fifteenth century.

John William Dell *c.* 1905. Known as Will, he was one of Beryl's brothers. He is seen here in costume for the St Albans Fair.

Taking part in a pageant *c*. 1930. The three young actors here are from left to right: Reg Childs, May Matthews amd Vi Hagger.

A Young Flower *c*. 1930. Olive Foulder is dressed up as a flower for a village pageant.

Leverstock Green W.I. Pageant *c*. 1930. Some of the ladies appear to be rather on the large size! This was photographed on the tennis court next to the Parish Hall.

Monks from Leverstock Green, July 1950. Many of the local churches around Hemel Hempstead took part in the pageant to celebrate 800 years of St Mary's Church, Hemel. This contingent from Holy Trinity, including the Revd Thomas, made excellent monks.

Medieval ladies, July 1950. Not to be outdone by the men, the ladies and children of Holy Trinity Church also took part in St Mary's 800th anniversary celebrations. Included in the photo are Marjorie Thomas, Madge Field, Jill Parkins and Barbara Aldous.

The weekly dancing class c. 1946. Mr and Mrs Fred Leat held a weekly dancing class in the parish hall. Members of the local youth who attended the classes can be seen here on the tennis court next to the hall. Mrs Leat is on the far left of the first standing row, Mr Leat on the far right of the back row.

Drama in the parish hall *c*. 1950. Amateur dramatics have always been a feature of village life, and the tradition continues today with the Leverstock Green Amateur Dramatic Society, (LADS) and the Leverstock Green Players. Seen here is some of the local talent in a one act play.

L.G. Players present three plays, 22 and 23 November 1956. The casts were: *Chin-Chin Chinaman*: Reg Tothill, Margaret Anthony, Derek Bartaby; *The Bugginses' Picnic*: Arthur Miles, Marion Stockwell, Ann Squibb, Russell Matthews, Madge Field; *In a Glass Darkly*: Mary Gibson, Ross Beaumont, Molly Tothill, and Eileen Anthony.

W.I. flower stall, *c.* 1956. Margaret Shuffrey (left) and other members of the local WI manning their produce stall held in the Parish Hall. The coleus plant at the back only cost 1/6d!

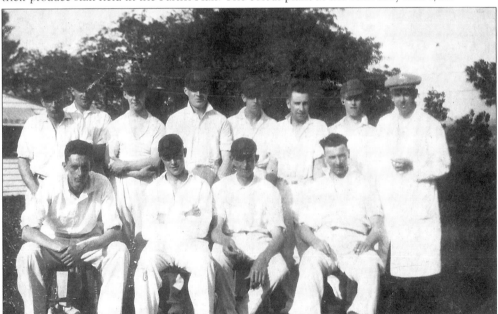

Leverstock Green cricket team, *c.* 1930. The team's ground was away from the village at Cherry Trees Farm, belonging to a member of the team, Bill Gale. Cows frequently had to be driven from the field and cow pats cleared away before a game could get underway. The team had a demon fast bowler, Albert Steers, who had a trial for the Middlesex County Eleven. Other members of the team included Sydney Dollimore and Arthur White.

Greenhills Cricket Club, 11 June 1949. Photographed at Rosedale Sports Club Cheshunt, from left to right, back row are: S. Rance (scorer), W. Ison, B. Field, J. Daniel, E. Hall, E. Milmer, E. Perkins(Umpire) and D.G. Dell. Centre row: C. Allard, J. King, R. Childs (captain), S. Miller. In the front were: P. Rogers and G. Latchford. Leverstock Green now has its own ground and pavilion on the Green.

Leverstock Green Football Club, 1907. Notice the strange arrangement of shin pads over the socks.

Leverstock Green Football Club *c*. 1910.

Leverstock Green Football Team, 1932. From left to right, front row: J. Mayo, J. Matthews, G. Faulder. Central row: S. Odell, F. Missenden, F. Kerry, H. Briggs. Back row: G. Tompkins, W. Whitman, S. Minter, F. Waldron, E. Perry.

110

Leverstock Green Football Team *c*. 1937. Front row, from left to right: S. Odell, J. Cooley, D. Baker, J. Matthews, V. Hosier, P. Rance. Back row: E. Perry, R. Ellis, B. Wooton, W. Hughes, S. Hall, E. Final, J. Cooley (Senior).

Leverstock Green Football Team, 1956-57. Front row, from left to right: L. Hooker, R. Spurr, L.Collier, B. Vaughan, B. Bullock, J. Matthews. Back row: A. Miles, K. Hoar, J. Lockyer, E. Milmer, J. Hemley, J. Francis, P. Blaxhill, F. Holloway, C. Rowe.

Tennis stars open New Village tennis court c. 1948. Replacing the old grass court, a new hard court was built at the side of the parish hall. Left to right are: Davis Cup player N. R. Lewis, past England player C.J. Hovell, Dr. J.C. Gregory, a village resident who was also the then non-playing captain of the Davis Cup team, and F. A. Jarvis, the Captain of Hertfordshire.

Winners of the Leverstock Green Tennis Tournament, 7 September 1956. The mens' singles winner was Ted Milmer (left), the ladies singles winner Madge Field, who also won the mixed doubles with her husband Bernard. They were presented with their trophies in the Parish Hall. The Tennis Club is now situated off Grassmere Close and has twelve all weather courts.

Eight

Village Folk

Enjoying a smoke *c.* 1910. These village worthies enjoy a hard earned rest from their labours. William Parkins the fishmonger is in the centre.

The Fishmonger's round *c*. 1900. William Parkins (centre) was the village's fishmonger from at least 1885 until his death in 1916. After purchasing the fish daily, it was cleaned and prepared at the family home in Westwick Row (see page 35) before being delivered by pony cart. His son Tom (right) accompanied him.

William and Lydia Parkins *c*. 1914. Photographed outside their home, the couple are wearing their best clothes. Lydia's gown appears in the family's wedding photos (see page 98).

Lydia Parkins with her sons *c.* 1930. From left to right, they are Harry, Cecil, Fred and Walter.

At the bar of the Leather Bottle *c.* 1945. Cecil Parkins eventually took over the licence of the pub from his mother-in-law when she retired in 1945.

A chat with the landlord, Cecil Parkins *c*. 1955. Notice the changes in these photographs.

Olive and Cecil Parkins Retire, December 1964. For most of the time since their marriage in 1921, the couple had made the Leather Bottle their home, retiring to nearby Hunton Bridge. As well as being behind the bar at the Leather Bottle, Cecil had been Chairman of the Football Club until earlier in 1964, and Olive was a founder member of the local WI.

Four generations *c*. 1935. Granny Dell, (née Elizabeth Seaman) in the wheelchair, has her step-daughter Lily Seabrook behind her, Lily's daughter Olive Parkins to her right, and Olive's daughter Madge to her left. In 1543 a Giles Dell lived in Westwick Row; Elizabeth's husband John was his descendant.

Sheep on the Green, *c*. 1944. Young Jill Parkins, youngest daughter of Olive and Cecil Parkins, enjoyed stroking the local shepherd's dog. It is easy to see from this picture how relatively small the green used to be. The hedge behind the sheep bordered North End Farm and the cottages were attached to Blacksmiths Row.

Outside The Leather Bottle *c*. 1910. On the right is the wheelright, Robert William Wright, who had his workshop next to the pub and was also the undertaker and parish clerk. Behind him is Walter Parkins the fishmonger and to his right are probably Arthur and Lily Seabrook who ran the pub. By the van are Tom and Will Parkins.

Sybil and Olive Seabrook, *c*. 1920. Brought up at The Leather Bottle, the sisters frequently dressed alike, although presumably in this photograph they are dressed alike because they are to be bridesmaids.

John Dell *c*. 1900. A hay dealer, he was born in 1848. He was the father of Lily Seabrook, by his first marriage.

More Dells, Christmas 1926. Left to right: Hilda Chambers (née Dell), Marie Elizabeth (her daughter), Beryl, Mary Olive, and their mother Elizabeth, wife of John Dell (above) and known as Granny Dell.

Possibly Leverstock Green's first car *c*. 1919. Owned by Edmund Perkins, it was used as a taxi to Boxmoor Station (see page 13).

Thomas Steers, 18 February 1919.

Susan and Arthur Clark *c.* 1924. Mother and son can be seen here outside the house next to the Leather Bottle in which the family rented two rooms. The property was demolished when the Village Centre was redeveloped in the early 1960s.

Gravel pit workers *c.* 1924. This gang of men, which included Arthur Clark (above) worked in the gravel pit near to 'The Dells'.

Three Friends, 1928. Photographed in the grounds of the school house in 1928 are: seated, Olive Foulder, and behind her to the left Vera Windsor, and to the right Doris Cox.

May Matthews c. 1938. The Matthews family lived in one of the cottages in Blacksmiths Row, outside which this was taken. The petrol pumps of The Three Horseshoes Garage can clearly be seen behind May.

Charles William Matthews *c*. 1915. Known as Willy or Bill, he was one of May's brothers. Sadly he died in hospital at the age of 13 after a shot gun wound to his leg went gangrenous. The wound was a result of an accident which occurred in the cherry orchard in Bedmond Road.

Mrs Matthews *c*. 1948. Mrs Matthews was a familiar sight on the green where she grazed her geese, rounding them up each night and locking them in.

Mr and Mrs Woodwards c. 1900. The Woodwards lived at Mafeking Villas, (see page 24).

Francis Haviland (left), was companion to Gladys (Betty) Shuffrey (right) of Leverstock Green Farm.

The Blacksmith, late 1930s. Arthur Mears was the village blacksmith from c. 1908. As well as this, he was also an excellent calligrapher and often got called upon to use these skills. He was the last village blacksmith, bringing to an end a tradition at least 250 years old.

Mrs Mears, c. 1940, the blacksmith's wife.

Village postmaster, *c.* 1948. Mr Haynes took over the village shop and post office after Mr and Mrs R.F. Houston moved to Norfolk in November 1945. The Houstons had run the post office and shop for fourteen years.

Edward Goodman *c.* 1940. The Goodmans lived at The Rose and Crown and emigrated to Tasmania *c.* 1952. Here he can be seen plucking a goose for Christmas at Leverstock Green Farm where he used to help out.

In the parish hall *c.* 1960. Mr and Mrs Plain are seated on the right, with Mrs Louise Field seated to the far left. Mrs Nesta Buglas is standing next to Mrs Field. The Parish Hall (a timber hut) was built at the corner of Pancake Lane after a trust was set up in 1915 to establish a meeting place and function room for the residents of the parish. The sale of the land in 1987 led to the establishment of the present Leverstock Green Parish Trust in 1992.

Acknowledgements

There are many people without whom this book would never have materialised. In particular I would like to give very special thanks to the Leverstock Green Parish Trust for their sponsorship and encouragement; to Tony and Margaret Shuffrey, Terry Crickmore, Jo Gilbert, and Raymond Weaver for their help in reproducing photographs; and to Jo Page for photographing those pictures in The Plough which couldn't be removed from the wall.

Considerable help and encouragement also came from the two local Primary School headmasters, John Fellows (Leverstock Green), and Martin Lynch (Hobbs Hill Wood); and from Peter and Elaine Webber of CellPath Plc, Leverstock Green Farm.

I would also like to thank my husband Martin, and my sons Owen and Alex for their understanding and help, for putting up with my preoccupation with 'old Leverstock Green', and for solving any problems which occurred with my computer. Without their appreciation, interest and support, the research necessary for this book would not have been possible. Special thanks go to my step-father Fred Gowan, for reading through my script and making helpful comments.

In addition many people have delved in their archives, drawers, cupboards and albums to find the prints which make up this book. I am deeply grateful to them for allowing me to reproduce them here. They are: Revd Michael Abbott (Holy Trinity, Leverstock Green), Audrey Baillie, Rita Bromley, Barry Bruce, Olive Campbell, Mary Clarke, Mary Cole, Rose Colclough, Commission for the New Towns, Margaret Cox, Mr Graham Crawford, Madge Field, The Francis Frith Collection, *The Gazette* Hemel Hempstead, Cynthia Groves, *Herts Advertiser*, Bob and Phyllis Ison, William Henry John, Maureen Kelly, Joseph Lawson, Leverstock Green Football Club, Mrs Luby, Martin Lynch: Headmaster Hobbs Hill Wood Primary School, Jill Ray, Winnifred Read, Chris Reynolds, Steve Robinson, Jackeline Rogers, A.L. Shuffrey, Revd Peter Stokes, Marie Thomas, and May Williamson. Thanks are also due to Sydney Dollimore for sharing his wonderful reminiscences of the village in times past.

It has not always proved possible to trace everyone who holds the copyright to some of the material. Whilst every effort has been made to do so, I must apologise to anyone from whom I was unable to seek permission to publish.

The information contained in the introduction and captions was gleaned in part from the individuals above, and from the research I have undertaken over the past two years into the history of Leverstock Green. In the course of my researches I have referred to many different sources, a full list of which is available in the file on *The Leverstock Green Chronicle* held at Leverstock Green Library. Many of these sources were original documents held at the Hertfordshire Record Office, and I would like to express my gratitude to all the staff there for the help they have given and continue to give me.

This book is dedicated to the memory of Terry Crickmore, who died suddenly on 29 July 1995, and who was a great help to me in putting together this collection of old photographs.

Barbara Chapman, February 1996